TRANSLATED KINGDOMS
SCOTTISH POEMS OF THE SEA

TRANSLATED KINGDOMS

SCOTTISH POEMS OF THE SEA

Selected and introduced by
Jenni Calder

NMS Publishing

Published by NMS Publishing Limited, Royal Museum, Chambers Street, Edinburgh EH1 1JF

Collection © NMS Publishing Limited 1999

Information about our books is available at www.nms

British Library Cataloguing in Publication Data
A catalogue record of this book is available from the British Library

ISBN 1 901663 04 3

Designed by NMS Publishing
Printed in the United Kingdom by Cambridge University Press, Printing Division

Cover illustration: The Bay of Barrisdale in Loch Hourne from *A voyage round the North and North-West coast of Sotland and the adjacent islands...* by William Daniell, 1769-1837. By courtesy of the Library of National Museums of Scotland.

ACKNOWLEDGEMENTS

Intrusion of the Human by Norman MacCaig from *Collected Poems,* 1990 by permission of the Estate of Norman MacCaig and The Hogarth Press; Ian Hamilton Finlay for *Mansie Considers the Sea in the Manner of Hugh MacDiarmid* from *The Dancers Inherit the Party,* Fulcrum Press, 1969 and *The Boat's Blueprint* from *Poems to Hear and Sea,* Macmillan, 1971; Dilys Rose and Chapman for *Figurehead* from *Madame Doubtfire's Dilemma,* Chapman, 1989; Polygon for *Under the Pier* by Ian Stephen from *Varying States of Grace*; George Bruce for *Sumburgh Head* from *Collected Poems,* EUP; Christine De Luca for *Brekken Beach, Nort Yell* from *Voes and Sounds,* The Shetland Library, 1994; John Murray (Publishers) Ltd for *Sea Runes* and *Haddock Fisherman* by George Mackay Brown from *Selected Poems 1954-83* 1991; Scottish National Dictionary Association for *Arctic Convoy* by J K Annand; Carcanet Press Limited for *Photograph of Emigrants* and *The Drowned* by Iain Crichton Smith from *Collected Poems,* Carcanet, 1992, for *Shores* by Sorley Maclean from *Collected Poems,* 1989, for Burns Singer *SOS Lifescene* from *Selected Poems,* 1977, and for *Birlinn of Clanranald* by Alasdair MacMeister Alasdair, translated by Iain Crichton Smith from *The Poetry of Scotland* ed R Watson EUP, 1995; Derick Thomson for *Brown-haired Allan* by Ann Campbell, translated by Derick Thomson from *The Poetry of Scotland* ed R Watson; David Higham Associates for *The Alban Goes Out* by Naomi Mitchison from *The Cleansing of the Knife,* Canongate, 1978; *Children of Greenock* by W S Graham from *Collected Poems 1942-77,* Faber, 1979 © the Estate of W S Graham; Black Ace for *Sea-Changes* by David Daiches from *A Weekly Scotsman,* Black Ace, 1994; W L Lorimer Memorial Trust Fund for *The Two Neighbours* by George Campbell Hay.

Every effort has been made to trace copyright holders. If we have made errors or omissions we would be grateful to hear from the authors or publishers concerned.

CONTENTS

Introduction

Hugh MacDiarmid famously lamented the fact that Scotland is not entirely surrounded by water. There is, nevertheless, plenty of sea around Scotland, plenty of seashore and firths, islands and skerries, and lives and communities that have been shaped by the waves and the tides.

These poems reflect more than a thousand years of Scotland and the sea. The sea brought diverse peoples to Scotland's shores - settlers long before history was written down, Gaels from Ireland in the fifth century, Vikings from Scandinavia, Normans from France via England. Christianity crossed the sea from Ireland and over the centuries the sea took Scottish pilgrims and missionaries all over the world. The sea provided a political and economic highway to first Europe, then to the far east and far west. It was also the highway that took emigrants to new worlds. The sea was an essential ingredient of Scotland's industrial success. And the fish of the sea brought a livelihood to communities from Berwick to the Solway.

Many others have depended on the sea for a living: mariners and merchants, shipbuilders and ships' chandlers, harbour masters and holiday landladies, ferrymen and oil riggers, pirates and smugglers, coastguards and lighthouse keepers. The practical and economic impact of the sea on life in Scotland has been of huge proportions. But perhaps what these poems show most of all is the way the sea has entered the Scottish imagination and is essential to the pulse of Scottish culture. Some of the oceans in these poems are as metaphorical as they are real.

Many of the poems here have strong links with displays and objects in the Museum of Scotland. The gallery called *Na Gaidheil*, The Gael, is full of echoes of 'The Birlinn of Clanranald'. The Corrievreckin, title of Kate Whiteford's tapestry displayed near the Museum's entrance, features in John Leyden's 'The Mermaid'. The Firth of Forth, Lewis

Spence's 'Yon auld claymore', crops up all over the Museum, and Iain Crichton Smith's 'Photograph of Emigrants' could have been written for the gallery *Scotland and the World*. Robert Fergusson's 'Caller Oysters' are on the menu in *The Spirit of the Age*. The Stevenson family's lighthouses, celebrated in R L Stevenson's 'The Light-Keeper' and 'To my father', can be found in *The Workshop of the World*, where you will also find material linked with shipbuilding and the industries of the Clyde, evoked by W S Graham's 'The Children of Greenock'. J K Annand's 'Arctic Convoy' is a powerful link with the memories of the Second World War featured through objects in *Twentieth Century*. And there are many more connections.

The poems are introduced by Norman MacCaig's 'Intrusion of the Human', wonderfully evocative of the sea as a different and mysterious world, and defining a moment of human impact. This poem gives the collection its title, *Translated Kingdoms*, intended to suggest the realms of the sea transformed by human activity - including the imagination at work and the writing of poetry.

INTRUSION OF THE HUMAN

On the tiny sea, with an archipelago of two islands,
a breeze wanders aimlessly about,
snail-trailing over mucous water, depositing
small sighs on the sand.

A day for mermaids. A day for their inhuman eyes
and voices without vibrato. Shell mirrors
keep sinking from sight.

In the kingdom of fish whole parliaments are on the move
and guerrillas lurk
in the ruins and cellars of weed.

And in the history of light a peregrine
shoots from a sea cliff. Before its moment is over
a song will have ended, a flight
stalled in a zero of the air.

An implacable scenario – till
round the skulled headland a tiny sail
loafs into view. And everything
becomes its setting. Everything shrugs together
round a blue hull and a brown sail. Everything's changed
by the human voices carelessly travelling over
the responding water, through the translated kingdoms.

Norman MacCaig

MANSIE CONSIDERS THE SEA
IN THE MANNER OF HUGH MACDIARMID

The sea, I think, is lazy,
It just obeys the moon
– All the same I remember what Engels said:
'Freedom is the consciousness of necessity.'

Ian Hamilton Finlay

THE FISHERMAN'S SONG

O blithely shines the bonnie sun
Upon the Isle of May,
And blithely rolls the morning tide
Into St Andrew's Bay.

When haddocks leave the Firth of Forth,
And mussels leave the shore,
When oysters climb up Berwick Law,
We'll go to sea no more,
No more,
We'll go to sea no more.

Anon

CALLER HERRIN'

Wha'll buy my caller herrin'?
They're bonnie fish and halesome farin';
Wha'll buy my caller herrin',
New drawn frae the Forth?

When ye were sleepin' on your pillows,
Dreamed ye aught o' our puir fellows –
Darkling as they faced the billows,
A' to fill our woven willows?

Wha'll buy my caller herrin'?
They're no brought here without brave daring:
Buy my caller herrin',
Hauled through wind and rain.

Wha'll buy my caller herrin'?
Oh, ye may ca' them vulgar farin', –
Wives and mithers, 'maist despairin',
Ca' them lives o' men.

When the creel o' herrin passes,
Ladies clad in silks and laces
Gather in their braw pelisses,
Cast their necks, and screw their faces.

Caller herrin's no got lightly;
Ye can trip the spring fu' tightly;
Spite o' tauntin', flauntin', flingin',
Gow has set you a' a-singin.

Neebour wives, now tent my tellin:
At ae word be in your dealin', –
Truth will stand when a' thing's failin'.

Carolina Oliphant, Lady Nairne

PIRATE STORY

Three of us afloat in the meadow by the swing,
   Three of us aboard in the basket on the lea.
Winds are in the air, they are blowing in the spring,
   And waves are on the meadow like the waves there are at sea.

Where shall we adventure, today that we're afloat,
   Wary of the weather and steering by a star?
Shall it be to Africa, a-steering of the boat,
   To Providence, or Babylon, or off to Malabar?

Hi! but here's a squadron a-rowing on the sea –
   Cattle on the meadow a-charging with a roar!
Quick and we'll escape them, they're mad as they can be,
   The wicket is the harbour and the garden is the shore.

R L Stevenson

The Firth

Yon auld claymore the Firth o' Forth,
Yon richt Ferrara o' the North,
Upon whase steel the broon sails scud,
Staining the blade like draps o' bluid,
Lies drawn betwixt the North and South,
A sword within the Lyon's mouth.
And in yon fell chafts shall it lie
Sae lang as there is Albanie,
Stapping the roar o' meikle jaws,
Point tae the hert and hilt to paws
O' yon auld rampart, girning baste
Wha o' cauld steel luves best the taste.

Like tae a watter on a wab
Woven wi' silks o' gowd and drab,
Scamander on a palace wall
Shone never mair majestical,
And like a castel sewn in soye
The turrets o' the Scottish Troy
Atowre that meikle moat rise up
Like weirds abune a witch's cup -
A wondrous ferlie frae the sea
Warth a hale warld o' poesie!

Lewis Spence

SIR PATRICK SPENS

The king sits in Dunfermline toune,
 Drinking the blude-reid wine:
'O whar will I get guid sailor,
 To sail this ship of mine?'

Up and spake an eldern knicht,
Sat at the kings richt knee:
'Sir Patrick Spens is the best sailor
That sails upon the sea.'

The king has written a braid letter,
And signed it wi his hand,
And sent it to Sir Patrick Spens,
Was walking on the sand.

The first line that Sir Patrick red,
A loud lauch lauched he;
The next line that Sir Patrick red,
The tear blinded his ee.

'O wha is this has don this deid,
This ill deid don to me,
To send me out this time o' the year,
To sail upon the sea.

'Mak haste, mak haste, my merry men all,
Our guid ship sails the morn.'
'O say not sae, my master dear,
For I fear a deadly storm.

'Late yestreen I saw the new moon,
Wi the auld moon in her arm,
And I fear, I fear, my dear master,
That we will come to harm.'

O our Scots nobles were richt laith
To weet their cork-heeled shoon;
Bot lang owre a' the play were played,
Their hats they swam aboon.

O lang, lang may their ladies sit,
Wi their fans into their hand,
Or ere they see Sir Patrick Spens
Come sailing to the land.

O lang, lang may the ladies stand,
Wi their gold cems in their hair,
Waiting for their ain dear lords,
For they'll see them na mair.

Half owre, half owre to Aberdour,
It's fifty fadom deep,
And their lies guid Sir Patrick Spens,
Wi the Scots lords at his feet.

Anon

CALLER OYSTERS

Happy the man who, free from care and strife,
In silken or in leathern purse retains
A splendid shilling. He nor hears with pain
New oysters cry'd, nor sighs for chearful ale.
                              Philips

Of a' the waters that can hobble
A fishin yole or salmon coble,
And can reward the fishers trouble,
                Or south or north,
There's nane sae spacious and sae noble
                As Firth of Forth.

In her skate and codlin sail,
The eil fou souple wags her tail,
Wi' herrin, fleuk, and mackarel,
                And whitens dainty:
Their spindle-shanks the labsters trail,
                Wi partans plenty.

Auld Reikie's sons blyth faces wear;
September's merry month is near,
That brings in Neptune's caller chere,
                New oysters fresh;
the halesomest and nicest gear
                Of fish or flesh.

O! then we needna gie a plack
For dand'ring mountebank or quack,
Wha o' their drogs sae bauldly crack,
        And spred sic notions,
As gar their feckless patient tak
        Their stinkin potions.

Come prie, frail man! For gin thou art sick,
The oyster is a rare cathartic,
As ever doctor patient gart lick
        To cure his ails;
Whether you hae the head or heart-ake,
        It ay prevails.

Ye tiplers, open a' your poses,
Ye wha are faush'd we' plouky noses,
Fling owr your craig sufficient doses,
        To fleg awa' your simmer roses,
        And naething under.

Whan big as burns the gutters rin,
Gin ye hae catcht a droukit skin,
To Luckie Middlemist's loup in,
        And sit full snug
O'er oysters and a dram o' gin,
        Or haddock lug.

When auld Saunt Giles, at aught o'clock,
Gars merchant lowns their chopies lock,
There we adjourn wi' hearty fock
      To birle our bodles,
And get wharewi' to crack our joke
        And clear our noddles.

Whan Phoebus did his windocks steek,
How aften at that ingle cheek
Did I my frosty fingers beek,
       And taste gude fare?
I trow there was nae hame to seek
       Whan steghin there.

While glaikit fools, o'er rife o' cash,
Pamper their weyms wi' fousom trash,
I think a chiel may gayly pass;
       He's no ill boden
That gusts his gabb wi' oyster sauce,
       And hen weel soden.

At Musselbrough, and eke Newhaven,
The fisher wives will get top livin,
When lads gang out on Sunday's even
      To treat their joes,
And tak of fat pandours a prieven,
       Or mussel brose:

Than sometimes 'ere they flit their doup,
They'll ablins a' their siller coup
For liquor clear frae cutty stoup,
   To weet their wizen,
And swallow o'er a dainty soup,
   For fear they gizzen.

A' ye wha canna stand sae sicker,
Whan twice you've toom'd the big ars'd bicker,
Mix caller oysters wi' your liquor,
   And I'm your debtor,
If greedy priest or drouthy vicar
   Will thole it better.

Robert Fergusson

from THE ANTIQUARY

The herring loves the merry moonlight
 The mackerel loves the wind,
But the oyster loves the dredging sang,
 For they come of a gentle kind.

Quoted by *Sir Walter Scott*

The Baltic

'Whaur are gaen sae fast, my bairn,
  It's no tae the schule ye'll win?'
'Doon tae the shore at the fit o' the toon
  Tae bide till the brigs come in.'

'Awa' noo wi' ye and turn ye hame,
  Ye'll no hae time tae bide;
It's twa lang months or the brigs come back
  On the lift o' a risin' tide.

'I'll sit me doon at the water's mou'
  Till there's niver a blink o' licht,
For my feyther bad' me tae tryst wi' him
  In the dairkness o' yesternicht.

'Rise ye an' rin tae the shore,' says he,
  At the cheep o' the waukin bird,
And I'll bring ye a tale o' a foreign land
  The like that ye niver heard.'

'Oh, haud yer havers ye feckless wean,
  It was but a dream ye saw,
For he's far, far north wi' the Baltic men
  I' the hurl o' the Baltic snaw;

And what did he ca' yon foreign land?'
  'He tell'tna its name tae me,
But I doot it's no by the Baltic shore,
  For he said there was nae mair sea.'

Violet Jacob

FIGUREHEAD

The fog thickens.
I see no ships.
The gulls left days ago

Ebbing into the wake
Like friends grown tired
Of chasing failure.

I miss their uncouth snatch and grab
Their loud insatiable hunger.
I see nothing but fog.

Before my ever-open eyes
The horizon has closed in
The world's end dissolved.

I lumber on, grudging my status -
I'm purpose-built to dip and toss
My cleavage, crudely carved

To split waves
My hair caked with salt
My face flaking off.

Dilys Rose

from THE SHIPWRECK

Fierce and more fierce the gathering tempest grew,
South, and by west, the threatening demon blew:
The ship no longer can her top-sails spread,
And every hope of fairer skies is fled.
Bow-lines and halyards are cast off again,
Clue-lines hauled down, and sheets let fly amain:
Embrailed each top-sail, and by braces squared,
The seamen climb aloft and man each yard:
They furled the sails, and pointed to the wind
The yards, by rolling tackles then confined,
While o'er the ship the gallant boatswain flies;
Like a hoarse mastiff through the storm he cries.
Prompt to direct the unskilful still appears,
The expert he praises, and the timid cheers.
Now some, to strike top-gallant-yards attend,
Some, travellers up the weather-back-stays send,
At each mast-head the top-ropes others bend.
The parrels, lifts, and clue-lines soon are gone,
Topped and unrigged they down the back-stays run;
The yards secure along the booms were laid,
And all the flying ropes aloft belayed.
Their sails reduced, and all the rigging clear,
Awhile the crew relax from toils severe;
Awhile, their spirits with fatigue oppressed,
In vain expect the alternate hour of rest –
But with redoubling force the tempests blow,

And watery hills in dread succession flow:
A dismal shade o'ercasts the frowning skies,
New troubles grow, new difficulties rise;
No season this from duty to descend! –
'All hands on deck' must now the storm attend.

William Falconer

THE BOATIE ROWS

O weel may the boatie row,
And better may it speed;
And liesome may the boatie row
That wins the bairnies' bread.
The boatie rows, the boatie rows,
The boatie rows fu' weel;
And meikle luck attend the boat,
The murlain and the creel.

I cuist my line in Largo Bay,
And fishes I caught nine;
There's three to boil, and three to fry,
And three to bait the line.
The boatie rows, the boatie rows,
The boatie rows indeed;
And weel may the boatie row
That win's my bairnies' bread.

O weel may the boatie row,
That fills a heavy creel,
And cleeds us a' frae tap to tae,
And buy our parritch meal.
The boatie rows, the boatie rows,
The boatie rows indeed;
And happy be the lot of 'a
That wish the boatie speed.

When Jamie vowed he wad be mine,
And won frae me my heart,
Oh meikle lighter grew my creel;
He swore we'd never part.
The boatie rows, the boatie rows,
The boatie rows fu' weel;
And meikle lighter is the load
When love bears up the creel.

My kertch I put upon my head,
And dressed myself fu' braw;
But dowie, dowie was my heart
When Jamie gaed awa'.
But weel may the boatie row,
And lucky be her part;
And lightsome be the lassie's care,
That yields an honest heart.

When sandy, Jock, and Janetie,
Are up, and gotten lear,
They'll help to gar the boatie row,
And lighten a' our care.
The boatie rows, the boatie rows,

The boatie rows fu' weel;
And lightsome be her heart that bears
The murlain and the creel.

When we are auld, and sair bowed down,
And hirplin at the door,
They'll row to keep us dry and warm,
As we did them before.
Then weel may the boatie row,
And better may it speed,
And happy be the lot of 'a
That wish the boatie speed.

John Ewen

from THE ANTIQUARY

Life ebbs from such old age, unmark'd and silent,
As the slow neap-tide leaves yon stranded galley.
Late she rock'd merrily at the least impulse
That wind or wave could give; but now her keel
Is settling on the sand, her mast has ta'en
An angle with the sky, from which it shifts not.
Each wave receding shakes her less and less,
Till, bedded on the strand, she shall remain
Useless as motionless.

Quoted by *Walter Scott*

THE VOYAGE OF COURT

Suppose the court you cheer and treats
And fortune on you shines and beats,
I rede you than war luve war lee,
Suppose you sail betwix twa sheets
Uthers has sailit als weil as ye.

Gif changes the wind, of force ye mon
Bowline hook haik and sheet hale on.
Therefore beware with an sharp blawar
Gif ye wise avise hereon.
And set your sail a little lower.
For gif ye hauld your sail oer strek
There may come bubs ye not suspek.
There may come contrairs ye not knaw.
There may come storms and cause a lek
That ye man cap be wind and waw.

And thocht the air be fair and stormless,
Yet there hauld not your sail oer press
For of hie lands there may come flags,
At Sanct Abbs Head and Buchan Ness,
And rive your foresail all in rags.

Be ye than vexit and at under,
Your friends will free and on you wonder.
Therefore beware with oer hie lands,

Sic flags may fail. Suppose a hunder
Were you to help - they have no hands.

Dread this danger good friend and brudcr,
And tak example before of other.
Knaw courts and wind has oft sys variet.
Keep weil to your course and rule your rudder
And think with kings ye are not marriet.

Quentin Shaw

from ALMAE MATRES

St Andrews by the Northern Sea,
A haunted town it is to me!
A little city, worn and gray,
The gray North Ocean girds it round,
And oer the rocks, and up the bay,
The long sea-rollers surge and sound.
And still the thin and biting spray
Drives down the melancholy street,
And still endure, and still decay,
Towers that the salt winds vainly beat.
Ghost-like and shadowy they stand
Dim mirrored in the wet sea-sand.

Andrew Lang

OVERDUE

O ragin' wind
An' cruel sea,
Ye put the fear
O' daith on me.
I canna sleep,
I canna pray,
But prowl aboot
The docks a' day,
An' pu' my plaid
Aboot me ticht.
'Nae news yet, mistress!'
Ae mair nicht!

Helen B Cruickshank

TO SUFFIE
LAST OF THE BUCHAN FISHWIVES

A fish creel wi a wife aneth't
Steed at wir kitchen door.
A sma' quine grat at the wild-like shape
She'd nivver seen afore.

Ye cam fae anidder warl, Suffie,
Amo' hiz lan'ward folk,
The sough o the sea in the vera soun'
Of the words ye spoke.

Oor wyes warna yours, we nivver vrocht
Wi net nor line

Nor guttin knife, nor fan on haggert thoom
The stang o the brine.

We nivver hid to flee demintit
Tull the pier-heid,
Nor harken tull the heerican at midnicht,
Caul' wi dreid.

Spring efter Spring, or the teuchat's storm wis past
Ye wannert the road,
Heid tull the sleepy win' and boo't twa-faal,
Shoodrin yer load.

Simmer parks war kin'lier tull yer feet
Gin steens at styoo.
Bit fyles the stirkies chase't ye.
Fa wis feart? Them or you?

Yon bricht huddry buss that wis eence yer hair
Is grizzl't noo
An ower lang scannin o the sea his bleach't
Yer een's blue.

Wark an dule an widder sharpit yer face
Tull skin ower been.
As the tides tormint an futtle
A sma' fite steen.

Weel, umman, noo it's lowsin-time. We wuss
For you a fylie's ease;
Syne, at the hinmost wa'gyaan,
Quaet seas.

Flora Garry

THE LIGHT-KEEPER

1

The brilliant kernel of the night,
The flaming lightroom circles me:
I sit within a blaze of light
Held high above the dusky sea.
Far off the surf doth break and roar
Along bleak miles of moonlit shore,
Where through the tides the tumbling wave
Falls in an avalanche of foam
And drives its churned waters home
Up many an undercliff and cave.

The clear bell chimes: the clockworks strain,
The turning lenses flash and pass,
Frame turning within glittering frame
With frosty gleam of moving glass:
Unseen by me, each dusky hour
The sea-waves welter up the tower
Or in the ebb subside again;
And ever and anon all night,
Drawn from afar by charm of light,
A sea bird beats against the pane.

And lastly when dawn ends the night
And belts the semi-orb of sea,
The tall, pale pharos in the light
Looks white and spectral as may be.
The early ebb is out: the green
Straight belt of seaweed now is seen,

That round the basement of the tower
Marks out the interspace of tide;
And watching men are heavy-eyed,
And sleepless lips are dry and sour.

The night is over like a dream:
The sea-birds cry and dip themselves:
And in the early sunlight, steam
The newly bared and dripping shelves,
Around whose verge the glassy wave
With lisping wash is heard to lave;
While, on the white tower lifted high,
The circling lenses flash and pass
With yellow light in faded glass
And sickly shine against the sky.

2

As the steady lenses circle
With a frosty gleam of glass;
And the clear bell chimes,
And the oil brims over the lip of the burner,
Quiet and still at his desk,
The lonely Light-Keeper
Holds his vigil.

Lured from far,
The bewildered seagull beats
Dully against the lantern;
Yet he stirs not, lifts his head
From the desk where he reads,
Lifts not his eyes to see

The chill blind circle of night
Watching him through the panes.
This is his country's guardian,
The outmost sentry of peace.
This is the man
Who gives up that is lovely in living
For the means to live.

Poetry cunningly gilds
The life of the Light-Keeper,
Held on high in the blackness
In the burning kernel of night.
The seaman sees and blesses him,
The Poet, deep in a sonnet,
Numbers his inky fingers
Fitly to praise him.
Only we behold him,
Sitting, patient and stolid,
Martyr to a salary.

R L Stevenson

Arctic Convoy

Intil the pitmirk nicht we northwart sail
Facin the bleffarts and the gurly seas
That ser' out muckle skaith to mortal men.
Whummlin about like a waukrife feverit bairn
The gude ship snowks the waters o a wave,
Swithers, syne pokes her neb intil the air,
Hings for a wee thing, dinnlin, on the crest,
And clatters in the trouch wi sic a dunt
As gey near rives the platin frae her ribs
And flypes the tripes o unsuspectin man.

Northwart, aye northwart, in the pitmirk nicht.
A nirlin wind comes blawin frae the ice,
Plays dirdum throu the rails and shrouds and riggin,
Ruggin at bodies clawin at the life-lines.
There's sic a rowth o air that neb and lungs
Jist canna cope wi sic a dirlin onding.

Caulder the air becomes, and snell the wind,
The waters, splairgin as she dunts her boo,
Blads in a blatter o hailstanes on the brig
And geals on guns and turrets, masts and spars,
Cleedin the iron and steel wi coat o ice.

Northwart, aye northwart, in the pitmirk nicht.
The nirlin wind has gane, a lownness comes;

The lang slaw swall still minds us o the gale.
Restin aff-watch, a-sweein in our hammocks,
We watch our sleepin messmates' fozy braith
Transmogrify to ice upon the skin
That growes aye thicker on the ship-side plates.
Nae mair we hear the lipper o the water,
Only the dunsh o ice-floes scruntin by;
Floes that in the noon-day gloamin licht
Are lily-leafs upon my lochan dubh.
But nae bricht lily-flouer delytes the ee,
Nae divin bird diverts amang the leafs,
Nae sea-bird to convoy us on our gait.
In ilka deid-lown airt smools Davy Jones,
Ice-tangle marline spikes o fingers gleg
To claught the bodies o unwary sailors
And hike them doun to stap intil his kist.
Whiles 'Arctic reek' taks on the orra shapes
O ghaistly ships-o-war athort our gait,
Garrin us rin ram-stam to action stations
Syne see them melt awa intil the air.

Owre lang this trauchle lasts throu seas of daith
Wi ne'er a sign o welcome at the port,
Nae 'Libertymen fall in!' to cheer our herts
But sullen sentries at the jetty-heid
And leesome lanesome waitin at our birth.

At length we turn about and sail for hame
Back throu rouch seas, throu ice and snaw and sleet,
Hirdin the draigelt remnants o our flock
Bieldin them weel frae skaith o enemie.
But southwart noo we airt intil the licht
Leavin the perils o the Arctic nicht.

J K Annand

THE GREAT SILKIE OF SULE SKERRY

An earthly nourris sits and sings,
    And aye she sings, 'Ba, lily wean!
Little ken I my bairnis father
    Far less the land that he staps in.'

Then ane arose at her bed-fit,
    An a grumly guest I'm sure was he:
'Here am I, thy bairnis father
    Although that I be not comelie.

'I am a man, upo the lan,
    An I am a silkie in the sea;
And when I'm far and far frae land
    My dwelling is in Sule Skerrie.'

'It was na weel,' quo the maiden fair,
    It was na weel, indeed,' quo she,
'That the Great Silkie of Sule Skerrie
    Suld hae come and aught a bairn to me.'

Now he has taen a purse of goud.
    And he has pat it upo her knee,
Sayin, 'Gie to me my little young son,
    An tak thee up thy nourris-fee.

'An it sall come to pass on a simmer's day,
    When the sin shines het on evera stane,
That I will tak my little young son,
    And teach him for to swim the faem.

'An thu sall marry a proud gunner
    An a proud gunner I'm sure he'll be,
An the very first schot that ere he schoots
    He'll schoot baith my young son and me.'

Anon

Earl Rögnvald lands in Shetland
from the Orkneyinga Saga

Both my ships on beach went crashing;
When the surges swept my men off,
Sore afflicted by the billows
Were the friends of Hjalp and Fífa.
Surely this misadventure
Of the danger-seeking rovers
Will not soon be quite forgotten
By those who got such a wetting.

Anon, translated by Jon A Hjaltalin and Gilbert Goudie

Sumburgh Head

Rummle an' dunt o' watter,
Blatter, jinkin, turn an' rin –
A' there – burst an' yatter
Sea soun an' muckle an' sma win
Heich abune purpie sea, abune reid
Rocks – skraichs. That an' mair's the dirdit
Word – Sumburgh, Sumburgh Heid.

George Bruce

BREKKEN BEACH, NORT YELL

A mile aff we catch a glisk
o Brekken beach: webbed
atween headlands, a glansin arc
o ancient shalls
sun sillered.

Waves aff Arctic floes
bank in; dey shade fae cobalt
tae a glacial green; swall
an brack, rim on rim
o lipperin froad.

We rin owre dunes
crumplin smora,
fling aff wir shön
birze sand trowe taes
dell an bigg it;
shaste da doon draa
o da waves, loup
der hidmost gasps.

Abune wis, solan plane an plummet
an on da cliff, a tystie
triggit up in black and white
gawps at wir foally.

Da sun draps doon ahint his keep
an we man leave
an Eden aert
ta him.

Christine De Luca

Kalf Arnason fights for Earl Thorfinn against Earl Rognvald

From the Orkneyinga Saga

Have ye heard how Kalfr followed
Finnr's son in battle?
Quickly didst thou push thy vessels
'Gainst the Earl's ships on the water.
To destroy the son of Brusi,
Thou, courageous ship's commander,
Wast unwilling, but of hatred
Mindful, didst thou help Thorfinn.

When the Earls joined in battle
Misery there was unbounded.
Thick and fast the men were falling
In the struggle; sad the hour when
Nearer went the daring Eastmen
To the unexampled fire-rain.
In that battle off the Red Biorg
Many a noble man was wounded.

Swarthy shall become the bright sun,
In the black sea shall the earth sink,
Finished shall be Austri's labour,
And the wild sea hide the mountains,
Ere there be in those fair Islands
Born a chief to rule the people –
May our God both help and keep them –
Greater than the lost Earl Thorfinn.

Anon, translated by Jon A Hjaltalin and Gilbert Goudie

SEA RUNES

Five crags
The five black angels of Hoy
That fishermen avoid –
The Sneuk, The Too, The Kame, Rora, The Berry.

Elder
Charlag who has read the prophets
A score of times
Has thumbed the salt book also, wave after wave.

Crofter-Fisherman
Sea-plough, fish-plough, provider
Make orderly furrows.
The herring will jostle like August corn.

Shopkeeper
Twine, sea stockings, still to pay
And Howie trading
Cod for rum in the ale-house.

New Boat
We call this boat *Pigeon*.
Go gentle, dove
Among skuas, easterlies, reefs, whalebacks.

Fishmonger
The fishmonger stood at the rock
With bits of dull silver
To trade for torrents of uncaught silver.

George Mackay Brown

IN ORKNAY

Upon the utmost corners of the warld,
and on the borders of this massive round,
quhaire fates and fortoune hither hes me harld,
I doe deplore my greiffs upon this ground;
and seing roring seis from roks rebound
by ebbs and streames of contrair routing tyds,
and phebus chariot in their waves ly dround,
quha equallye now night and day divyds,
I cal to mynde the storms my thoughts abyde,
which ever wax and never dois decress,
for nights of dole dayes joys ay ever hyds,
and in their vayle doithal my weill suppress:
so this I see, quhaire ever I remove,
I change bot sees, bot can not chainge my love.

William Fowler

from TO CHARLES, DUKE OF BUCCLEUCH

Or would you be pleased but to fancy a whale,
And direct me to send it by sea or by mail,
The season I'm told is nigh over but still
I could get you one fit for the lake at Bowhill.
Indeed as to whales there's no need to be thrifty
Since one day last fortnight two hundred & fifty
Pursued by seven Orkney-men's boats and no more
Between Triffness and Liffness were driven on the shore. —
For this mighty shoal of leviathans lay
On our lee-beam a mile, in the loop of the bay
And the islemen of Sanda were all at the spoil
And flinching (so term it) the blubber to boil.
(Ye spirits of lavender drown the reflection
That awakes at the thoughts of this odorous dissection.)
To see this huge marvel fain would we go
But Wilson, the winds & the current said no.

Walter Scott

HADDOCK FISHERMEN

Midnight. The wind yawing nor-east.
A low blunt moon.
Unquiet beside quiet wives we rest.

A spit of rain and a gull
In the open door.
The lit fire. A quick mouthful of ale.

We push *Merle* at a sea of cold flame.
The oars drip honey.
Hook by hook uncoils under The Kame.

Our line breaks the trek of sudden thousands.
Twelve nobbled jaws,
Gray cowls, gape in our hands,

Twelve cold mouths scream without sound.
The sea is empty again.
Like tinkers the bright ones endlessly shift their ground.

We probe emptiness all the afternoon;
Unyoke; and taste
The true earth-food, beef and a barley scone.

Sunset drives a butcher blade
In the day's throat.
We turn through an ebb salt and sticky as blood.

More stars than fish. Women, cats, a gull
Mewl at the rock.
The valley divides the meagre miracle.

George Mackay Brown

UNDER THE PIER

It was a green world, under the pier.
Up there above, the dockers caught ropes
and metal boxes that had been tied to lorries
swung over the pier with
vegetables and fridges and wool
and chocolate biscuits.

We never walked when we went under but
chased a way down ladders of weedy metal
and then we leaped but
no-one ever fell in, that I remember.

It would have been a disgrace that,
if anyone's slip of a sandshoe had
sent them to splash the greenness
into wetness.
We'd have been surprised,
halted the game and
swapped looks copied from teachers,
ones that said,
'I'm disappointed in you.'

Ian Stephen

PHOTOGRAPH OF EMIGRANTS

Your faces cheerful though impoverished,
you stand at the rail, tall-collared and flat-capped.
You are leaving Lewis (Stornoway) behind.
Before you the appalling woods will rise
after the sea's sharp salt, your axes hack
the towering trunks. What are you leaving now? -
The calm routine of winding chimney smoke,
the settled village with its small sparse fields,
the ceilidhs and the narratives. Deceived
by chiefs and lairds, by golden promises,
you set off, smiling towards a new world,
Canada with its Douglas firs and snow,
its miles of desolate emptiness.

        Why do I weep
to see these faces, thin and obsolete,
these Sunday ties and collars, by the rail,
as the ship moves, and you move with it,
towards your flagrant destinies of sharp
bony starvation, ruinous alcohol.

All shall be revealed but at this time
your faces blaze with earnestness, and joy,
as if you were coming home instead of leaving.
Nothing will save some, standing by the rail,

others will come home in tartan caps,
a fury of possessions, and a love
of what's disappeared forever when they left,
themselves not being able to be there and here,
and therefore growing differently towards pictures
which frame them where they stand, thus staring out
into the inscrutable waters of their fates.

Iain Crichton Smith

from THE BIRLINN OF CLANRANALD

So they raised the speckled sails
    wind-tight, towering.
They stretched the stiff ropes against
    her sudden flowering,
timbers of resin red
    tapering proudly.

They were knotted with fierce vigour,
    neatly, firmly,
through eyes of iron hooks
    and round the ring bolts.

Every rope of their equipment
    was adjusted.
Coolly each took his position
    as accustomed.

Windows of the heavens opened
    blue-grey, spotted,
with the banging of the tempest
    fierce and haughty.

The sea gathered round about it
    a black cloak,
a rough, ruffled, swarthy mantle
    of ill look.

It swelled to mountains and to valleys
    shaggy-billowed,
the matted lumpy waters rearing
    up to hillocks.

The blue waves were mouthing chasms,
    horned and brutish,
fighting each other in a pouring
    deathly tumult.

It needed courage to be facing
    such tall towerings
phosphoresecnt flashes sparking
    from each mountain.

Grey-headed wave-leaders towering
    with sour roarings,
their followers with smoking trumpets
    blaring, pouring.

When the ship was poised on wave crest
    in proud fashion
it was needful to strike sail
    with quick precision.

When the valleys nearly swallowed us
    by suction
we fed her cloth to take her up to
    resurrection.

The wide-skirted curving waters,
    bellowing, lowing,
before they even had approached you,
    you'd hear roaring,

sweeping before them the small billows,
    onward sheering.
There'd be a massive deathly water
    hard for steering.

When she would plunge from towering summits
    down pell-mell
almost the ship's heel would be bruised
    by the sea-floor's shells,

the ocean churning, mixing, stirring
    its abyss,
seals and huge sea creatures howling
    in distress.

Impetuous tumult of the waters,
    the ship's going,
sparking their white brains about
    an eeries snowing!

And they howling in their horror
    with sad features
pleading by us to be rescued,
    'Save your creatures.'

Every small fish in the ocean
    belly-white
by the rocking violent motion
    killed outright.

Stones and shell fish of the bottom
    on the surface
mown by the relentless threshing
    of the current.

Alasdair MacMaighstir Alasdair, translated by
Iain Crichton Smith

BROWN-HAIRED ALLAN, I WOULD
GO WITH YOU

I am devastated tonight!
I have no thought of love-making.

Brown-haired Allan, ò-hì, I would go with you,
Hi ri ri ri ibh ò hio hùg oirinn ò,
Brown-haired Allan, ò-hì, I would go with you.

Thinking only of the storms and the strength
     of the tempest
that would drive the men from the harbour.
Brown-haired Allan, darling sweetheart,
I heard that you had made the crossing
in the slim black boat built with oak,
and that you had landed in Man:
that would not be my choice of harbour
but rather Stiadair Sound in Harris
or Miavaig Loch among the hills.

Brown-haired Allan, my own darling,
I gave you my love as a youngster:
it is a sad tale I have tonight,
not of the death of the cattle in want,
but of the wetness of your shirt,
and of the porpoises tearing at you.
Though I had a foldful of cattle
I would care little for it now,
I would not wish a change of spouse,
better to be with you on the mountain-top.

Brown-haired Allan,
I heard that you had been drowned,
would that I were beside you,
on whatever rock or bank you came ashore,
in whatever heap of seaweed the high tide leaves you.
I would drink, whatever my kin say,
not of the red wine of Spain
but of your breast's blood, I would prefer that.

May God give payment to your soul
for what I had of your private talk,
for what I had of your goods without purchase,
lengths of speckled silk,
though I should never live to use them.
My prayer to God on His throne
that I should not go in earth or shroud,
in a hole in the ground or a secret place,
but in the place you went, Allan.

I am devastated tonight!

Ann Campbell, translated by Derick Thomson

Over the Water to Charlie

Come boat me o'er, come row me o'er,
　　Come boat me o'er to Charlie;
I'll gie John Ross another bawbie,
　　To ferry me over to Charlie.
　　　　We'll o'er the water and o'er the sea,
　　　　　We'll o'er the water to Charlie;
　　　　Come weal, come woe, we'll gather and go,
　　　　　And live and die wi' Charlie.

Weel, weel, I lo'e my Charlie's name,
　　Though some there be that abhor him;
But oh to see Auld Nick gaun hame,
　　And Charlie's foes before him!

I swear by moon and stars sae bright,
　　And the sun that glances early,
If I had twenty thousand lives,
　　I'd risk them a' for Charlie.

I once had sons, I now hae nane,
　　I bred them, toiling sairly;
And I wad bear them a' again,
　　And lose them a' for Charlie!

James Hogg

SING ME A SONG OF A LAD THAT IS GONE

Sing me a song of a lad that is gone,
  Say, could that lad be I?
Merry of soul he sailed on a day
  Over the sea to Skye.

Mull was astern, Rum on the port,
  Eigg on the starboard bow;
Glory of youth glowed in his soul;
  Where is that glory now?

Sing me a song of a lad that is gone,
  Say, could that lad be I?
Merry of soul he sailed on a day
  Over the sea to Skye.

Give me again all that was there,
  Give me the sun that shone!
Give me the eyes, give me the soul,
  Give me the lad that's gone!

Sing me a song of a lad that is gone,
  Say, could that lad be I?
Merry of soul he sailed on a day
  Over the sea to Skye.

Billow and breeze, islands and seas,
  Mountains of rain and sun,
All that was good, all that was fair,
  All that was me is gone.

R L Stevenson

SHORES

If we were in Talisker on the shore
where the great white mouth
opens between two hard jaws,
Rubha nan Clach and the Bioda Ruadh,
I would stand beside the sea
re-newing love in my spirit
while the ocean was filling
Talisker bay forever:
I would stand there in the bareness of the shore
until Prishal bowed his stallion head.

And if we were together
on Calgary shore in Mull,
between Scotland and Tiree,
between the world and eternity,
I would stay there till doom
measuring sand, grain by grain,
and in Uist, on the shore of Homhsta
in presence of that wide solitude,
I would wait there for ever,
for the sea draining drop by drop.

And if I were on the shore of Moidart
with you, for whom my care is new,
I would put up in a synthesis of love for you
the ocean and the sand, drop and grain.
And if we were on Mol Stenscholl Staffin

when the unhappy surging sea dragged
the boulders and threw them over us,
I would build the rampart wall
against an alien eternity grinding (its teeth).

Sorley MacLean, translated from the Gaelic

EALASAID

Here are the shores you loved,
The tumbling waters,
Curdling and foaming on Atlantic strands,
The ocean, gentian-blue beyond believing,
The clean white sands.

And here the ancient speech
You loved essaying,
Rising and falling like the wave-borne birds,
The cadences that wind and tide are weaving
Of Gaelic words.

And here the little crofts
With thatch stone-weighted,
You told me of, so often ere I came.
How strange, that I am here without you, grieving
Your loved, lost name.

O fairest, loveliest,
Of Tiree's daughters,
White sea-bird, frightened in the city smoke,
Of all you loved the most, Life seemed bereaving
You; and your heart broke.

Oh, sleep you soundly now,
Ealasaid darling,
Beneath the sandy turf on Tiree's shore.
No more your island home you need be leaving,
Be sad no more!

Helen B Cruickshank

from FINGAL BOOK VI

Thus they passed the night in the song; and brought
back the morning with joy. Fingal arose on the heath,
and shook his glittering spear in his hand. – He
moved first toward the plains of Lena, and we
followed like a ridge of fire. Spread the sail, said the
king of Morven, and catch the winds that pour from
Lena. – We rose on the wave with songs, and rushed,
with joy, through the foam of the ocean.

James Macpherson

from LATHMON: A POEM

Whither hast thou fled, O wind, said the king of
Morven? Dost thou rustle in the chambers of the
south, and pursue the shower in other lands? Why
dost thou not come to my sails? To the blue face of
my seas? The foe is in the land of Morven, and the
king is absent. But let each bind on his mail, and
each assume his shield. Stretch every spear over the
wave; let every sword be unsheathed.

James Macpherson

LOCHABER NO MORE

Farewell to Lochaber, and farewell, my Jean,
Where heartsome wi' her I ha'e mony a day been;
For Lochaber no more, Lochaber no more,
We'll may-be return to Lochaber no more.
These tears that I shed they are a' for my dear,
And no for the dangers attending on wier;
Though borne on rough seas to a far-distant shore,
May-be to return to Lochaber no more.

Though hurricanes rise, though rise every wind,
No tempest can equal the storm in my mind;
Though loudest of thunders on louder waves roar,
There's naething like leavin' my love on the shore.

To leave thee behind me my heart is sair pained,
But by ease that's inglorious no fame can be gained,
And beauty and love's the command of the brave,
And I maun deserve it before I can crave.

Then glory, my Jeanie, maun plead my excuse;
Since honour commands me, how can I refuse?
Without it I ne'er could have merit for thee,
And losing thy favour I'd better not be.
I gae, then, my lass, to win honour and fame,
And if I should chance to come glorious hame,
I'll bring a heart to thee, with love running o'er,
And then I'll leave thee and Lochaber no more.

Allan Ramsay

To My Father

Peace and her huge invasion to these shores
Puts daily home; innumerable sails
Dawn on the far horizon and draw near;
Innumerable loves, uncounted hopes
To our wild coasts, not darkling now, approach:
Not now obscure, since thou and thine are there,
And bright on the lone isle, the foundered reef,
The long, resounding foreland, Pharos stands.

These are thy works, O father, these thy crown;
Whether on high the air be pure, the shine
Along the yellowing sunset, and all night
Among the unnumbered stars of God they shine;
Or whether fogs arise and far and wide
The low sea-level drown – each finds a tongue
And all night long the tolling bell resounds:
So shine, so toll, till night be overpast,
Till the star vanish, till the sun return,
And in the haven rides the fleet secure.

In the first hour, the seaman in his skiff
Moves through the unmoving bay, to where the town
Its earliest smoke into the air upbreathes
And the rough hazels climb along the beach.
To the tugg'd oar the distant echo speaks.
The ship lies resting, where by reef and roost
Thou and thy lights have led her like a child.

This hast thou done, and I – can I be base?
I must arise, O father, and to port
Some lost, complaining seaman pilot home.

R L Stevenson

THE DROWNED

It is true that the drowned return to us.
In the blue eyes of children we see them,
in a slight eccentricity of gait.

They spring actively out of the water, seeming
smaller than they were, bearing
large smiles, corn-coloured crowns.

Where the rocks are and the crabs manipulate
their bodies like toy tanks
in waters green and teeming like soup

they arise, clear-winged, articulating
sons and grandsons of themselves, stumpy
authentic chimes,

echoes, reflections, shadowy
waves that speak through the new waves,
underwritings, palimpsests,

a ghost literature behind another one,
carbons that have faint imprints on them,
blue veils in a fresh breeze.

Iain Crichton Smith

THE ECHOING CLIFF

White gulls that sit and float
Each on his shadow like a boat,
Sandpipers, oystercatchers
And herons, those grey stilted watchers,
From loch and corran rise,
And as they scream and squawk abuse
Echo from wooded cliff replies
So clearly that the dark pine boughs,
Where goldcrests flit
And owls in drowsy wisdom sit,
Are filled with sea-birds and their cries.

Andrew Young

from THE VILLA BY THE SEA

Mine is that delightful villa,
    Sweetly nesting by the sea;
Yet I sigh for a scintilla
    Of the bliss it promised me.

Though a pleasant cottage orné,
    Rich in trellis-work and flowers,
Here to sit and end my journey,
    How could I beguile the hours?

Love of Nature is a duty,
    And I fain would love it more.
But I weary of the beauty
    I have seen for weeks before.

Lofty are the hills and regal,
    Still they are the hills of old;
And like any other sea-gull
    Is the sea-gull I behold.

Tiresome 'tis to be a dreamer.
    When will it be time to dine?
Oh, that almost stand-still steamer,
    How it crawls across the brine!

                              James Hedderwick

from THE MERMAID

Now, lightly poised, the rising oar
Disperses wide the foamy spray,
And echoing far oer Crinan's shore,
Resounds the song of Colonsay.

'Softly blow, thou western breeze,
Softly rustle through the sail.
Soothe to rest the furrowy seas
Before my love, sweet western gale.

'Where the wave is tinged with red,
And the russet sea-leaves grow,
Mariners with prudent dread,
Shun the shelving reefs below.

'As you pass through Jura's sound,
Bend your course by Scarba's shore.
Shun, O shun the gulf profound,
Where Corrievreckin's surges roar.

'If from that unbottomed deep,
With wrinkled form and writhed train,
Oer the verge of Scarba's steep,
The sea-snake heave his snowy mane;

'Unwarp, unwind his oozy coils,
Sea-green sisters of the main,
And in the gulf where ocean boils,
The unwieldy wallowing monster chain.

'Softly blow, thou western breeze,
Softly rustle through the sail.
Soothe to rest the furrowed seas
Before my love, sweet western gale.'

Thus all to soothe the chieftain's woe,
Far from the maid he loved so dear.
The song arose, so soft and slow,
He seemed her parting sigh to hear.

The lonely deck he paces oer,
Impatient for the rising day,
And still from Crinan's moonlight shore
He turns his eyes to Colonsay.

The moonbeams crisp the curling surge
That streaks with foam the ocean green;
While forward still the rowers urge
Their course, a female form was seen.

That sea-maid's form, of pearly light,
Was whiter than the downy spray,
And round her bosom, heaving bright,
Her glossy yellow ringlets play.

Borne on a foamy crested wave,
She reached amain the bounding prow.
Then clasping fast the chieftain brave,
She, plunging, sought the deep below.

John Leyden

THE TWO NEIGHBOURS

Two that through windy nights kept company,
two in the dark, two on the sea in the steering,
with aye one another's bow-wave and wake to see,
the neighbour's light away on the beam plunging and soaring.

Two on blind nights seeking counsel in turn –
'Where will we head now?' – sharing their care and labours,
spoke across plashing waters from stern to stern,
comrades in calm, fellows in storm, night-sea neighbours.

Dark and daybreak, heat and hail had tried
and schooled the two in the master glance for esteeming
the curve of the outgoing net, the set of the tide,
the drift of wind and sea, the airt where the prey was swimming.

Two on the sea. And the one fell sick at last,
'for he was weak, the soul, and old'. And the other
watched long nights by his bed, as on nights that were past
he watched from the stern for his light, sea-neighbour, in ill a brother.

Watched by the peep of a lamp long nights by his side;
brightened his mood, talking their sea-nights over;
followed him to Cill Aindreis* when he died,
and left him in peace in a lee that would feel no wind for ever.

George Campbell Hay

*Cill Aindreis: the graveyard of Tarbert Loch Fyne

from THE ALBAN GOES OUT

All at once the light,
The neighbour boat's light,
Winks, signals to us.
Alec has shot. Steady now.

They break out of dreams and gossip, run to their
                    places,
John Ritchie has the boat-hook, kneels, watches,
                    smiling, intent,
As Sandy steers for the dropped end of the ring-net
And the winkie, the tiny lamp,
Bobs on the jabble, hard to spear as a salmon.
John Ritchie has it!

Circling uptide, the ring-net surrounds the herring;
Both boats have their wheel-house lights to show that
                    they have shot,
For the fleet is close now, shouting from deck to deck,
Robbie has shot, MacBride has shot, have a care man,
The nets is easy torn!

There are other trades, in the towns, where a man
                    would be glad,
Eyeing his neighbour, if business there was bad.
He must claw at his neighbour's throat like dogs that
                    fight in the street
But all that thought should be far from us in the
                    Carradale fleet.

Men and engines grunting and hauling,
The nets dripping, the folds falling;
The spring-ropes jerking to the winches' creaking
Wind in by fathoms from their sea-deep seeking,
Steady and long like a preacher speaking.
But the flow of the net we must all lay hold on,
The cork-strung back-rope our hands are cold on.
As we thrash at the net the dead fish falling
Gleam and break from the tight mesh mauling,
Show what we'll get from the bag of the net!
And fierce and straining and shoulders paining
We drag it out from the sea's wild sprawling,
From the lit wet hammocks' twist and spin;
And the leaded sole-rope comes slumping in.

Naomi Mitchison

THE CHILDREN OF GREENOCK

Local I'll bright my tale on, how
She rose up white on a Greenock day
Like the one first-of-all morning
On earth, and heard children singing.

She in a listening shape stood still
In a high tenement at Spring's sill
Over the street and chalked lawland
Peevered and lined and fancymanned

On a pavement shouting games and faces.
She saw them children of all cries
With everyone's name against them bled
In already the helpless world's bed.

Already above the early town
The smoky government was blown
To cover April. The local orient's
Donkeymen, winches and steel giants

Wound on the sugar docks. Clydeside,
Webbed in its foundries and loud blood,
Binds up the children's cries alive.
Her own red door kept its young native.

Her own window by several sights
Wept and became the shouting streets.
And her window by several sights
Adored the even louder seedbeats.

She leaned at the bright mantle brass
Fairly a mirror of surrounding sorrows,
The sown outcome of always war
Against the wordperfect, public tear.

Brighter drifted upon her the sweet sun
High already over all the children
So chained and happy in Cartsburn Street
Barefoot on authority's alphabet.

Her window watched the woven care
Hang webbed within the branched and heavy
Body. It watched the blind unborn
Copy book after book of sudden

Elements within the morning of her
Own man-locked womb. It saw the neighbour
Fear them housed in her walls of blood.
It saw two towns, but a common brood.

Her window watched the shipyards sail
Their men away. The sparrow sill
Bent grey over the struck town clocks
Striking two towns, and fed its flocks.

W S Graham

THE LOWLANDS OF HOLLAND

My love he's built a bonnie ship, and set her on the sea,
With seven score guid mariners to bear her companie.
There's three score is sunk, and three score dead at sea;
And the lowlands of Holland ha'e twined my love and me.

My love he built another ship, and set her on the main,
And nane but twenty mariners for to bring her hame;
But the weary wind began to rise, and the sea began to rout;
My love, then, and his bonnie ship, turn'd withershins about.

There shall neither coif come on my head, nor kame come
                                        in my hair;
There shall neither coal nor candle-licht come in my bouir mair;
Nor will I love another man until the day I dee,
For I never loved a love but ane, and he's drown'd in the sea.

Oh, haud your tongue my daughter dear, be still and be content;
There are mair lads in Galloway, ye need na sair lament.
Oh! There is nane in Galloway, there's nane at a' for me;
For I never loved a love but ane, and he's drown'd in the sea.

Anon

SOS Lifescene

That plunging mast, nailed to a whirligig gale,
Shows its three sheer signs of drowning. Those crewed wet boards
Drag at the spray. Oceans drip backwards and forth
From the tall steel prow, those seamen, crouched that sail.

Crouched to climb: cling of the white wetnesses.
Heave of the sea's deep sheets, wheezing like twenty
Conferences stacked round tables, pressing
Processions, quarrel of kingdoms: pitch salt centre.

Out of it, down from it, hangs the electric shout,
None gooseflesh sparks breathing white out on the rabble
Of sweaty and swaggering gales. Held hard to the squabbling
Waters, to Save Our Souls the sounds fade out.

Yet steered, here steered, and over the sea's salt dregs
Set climbing forth, is crewed by the conscious and steered.
Wheeled in two knotted hands through the callous but prayer-
Breasting, heart-wresting hour, is ruddered with rags.

For the men, backed out to the bone, catch up on the past
In a straight line, like winter…the trees. Burn back
The barren courses, confront the naked mistake,
The embezzled hours accounted, the fake blot erased.

Talk yourself out of it! Out of it! Talk yourself! Talk!
And a death's click closes those offices foaming with grins.
That stoke-black lascar, damp and salt with work,
Looks through a lurch at the red wreck under his skin.

That engineer who's thistle-eyed for sleep
Circles the clock through goaded hoops and trances
To where she departs…to where she hurries…she dances…
The damp cellar and whisky…the heart in a heap…

SOS it repeats, repeats, told, retold.
Small white far cry for help as they kindle close
Together or blaze in a curse. For the storm grows
To death for the captain and the boy blown blue by the cold.

Corked nets and clinging baits, those sodden boards
Muscled about by their men, drag deep at the shoals
And their hooked catchings draw blood. But bite to the core!
There are nine white pips crying 'help' in a black bowl.

Seeds of the storm, quick fish, the intense alone
Of their human cry, where the storm bleats down like a ram
And the waves whinny away; where the smooth sky's brown
Blacks out, and the stars are dead and don't matter a damn.

What matters is the cry, the cry like a screw,
Sharp-oiled to turning, clean-cutting fish-silver through
And through the teak air,
A makeshift repetitive batter to riveting prayer.

Like stitching sails this windfall patches men.
Question to answer, push and heave and tug,
Thick-fibred needlework, an electric plug,
Nine cock-crows savage the air and cry us all home.

Burns Singer

HENRY MARTIN

In merry Scotland, in merry Scotland,
There lived brothers three.
And they did cast lots which of them should go
To turn robber upon the salt sea.

The lot it fell out upon Henry Martin,
The youngest of all the three,
That he should turn pirate all on the salt sea
To maintain his two brothers and he.

He had not been sailing three long winter's nights
Nor yet three short winter's days,
Before he espied a tall lofty ship
Bearing down on him straightway.

Hello, hello, cried Henry Martin,
How far are you going, says he.
I'm a rich merchant ship, for old England I'm bound,
Will you please for to let me pass free.

Oh no, oh no, cried Henry Martin,
Heave to and heave to, says he.
For I mean to take your flowing gold
Or send you to the bottom of the sea.

Then broadside for broadside and at it they went
And they fought for three hours and more,
Till at last Henry Martin gave her the death shot
And down to the bottom went she.

Bad news, bad news, my brave English boys,
Bad news to fair London town.
There's a rich merchant ship and she's cast away,
And all of her merry men drowned.

Anon

THE BOAT'S BLUEPRINT

water

Ian Hamilton Finlay

SEA-CHANGES

Bays, estuaries, beaches, rocks.
All round the coast
The varied ocean heaves and laps.
We are an island
Oppressed (redeemed?) by water
Circumjacent,
Ringed round by wrecks invisible,
Fishing boats, trading vessels, transports.
Julius Caesar, William the Conqueror,
Walter Scott sailing from Leith to Edinburgh
Or on his 1814 lighthouse trip,
Small lobster craft from Pittenweem,
Drifters from Ullapool or Peterhead,
Thames barges, tea clippers,
The great Armada swept to the north by storms,
Wives and children maist despairing
Watching doomed rock-bound boats
Without Grace Darling. Sea-girt
This island. In the night
Waves breaking on the shore awake no sleeper,
Rhythm of their restless movement
By habitude half-heard, unheeded.
And then
Seaside resorts, bathing machines once,
Sea-side landlady and martello tower,
Joke juxtaposition, yet how strange,

How strange the coastal prospect,
The sea-history,
How sad the break-break-break
On the cold grey stones,
And for Keats's pure ablution
Round these human shores
Pollution.

David Daiches

INDEX OF TITLES

Index of First Lines

Index of Poets and Translators

OTHER TITLES FROM NMS PUBLISHING

POETRY
Spirit of Flight – Aviation Poetry
Present Poets
Scotland and the World

SCOTLAND'S PAST IN ACTION SERIES
Fishing & Whaling
Sporting Scotland
Farming
Spinning & Weaving
Building Railways
Making Cars
Leaving Scotland
Feeding Scotland
Going to School
Going to Church
Scots in Sickness & Health
Going on Holiday
Going to Bed
Shipbuilding
Scottish Bicycles & Tricycles
Scotland's Inland Waterways

Forthcoming titles:
Engineering
Getting Married
Scottish Music Hall
Cinema in Scotland
Brewing

SCOTS LIVES SERIES
The Gentle Lochiel
Elsie Inglis
Miss Cranston
Mungo Park

Forthcoming titles:
Scottish Suffragettes
Scotland & Slavery

ANTHOLOGY SERIES
Treasure Islands
Scotland's Weather
Scottish Endings
The Thistle at War

ARCHIVE PHOTOGRAPHY SERIES
Bairns
Into the Foreground
To See Oursels

GENERAL
Scottish Coins
Tartan
Scenery of Scotland
Viking-age Gold & Silver of Scotland
The Scottish Home

Obtainable from all good bookshops or direct from NMS
Publishing Limited, Royal Museum, Chambers Street,
Edinburgh EH1 1JF.